FRANKENSTEIN'S MONSTER
AND SCIENTIFIC METHODS

BY CHRISTOPHER L. HARBO • ILLUSTRATED BY AÓN

Consultant:
Joanne K. Olson, PhD
Associate Professor
Science Education
Iowa State University
Ames, Iowa

CAPSTONE PRESS
a capstone imprint

Graphic Library is published by Capstone Press,
1710 Roe Crest Drive, North Mankato, Minnesota 56003
www.capstonepub.com

Library of Congress Cataloging-in-Publication Data
Harbo, Christopher L.
  Frankenstein's monster and scientific methods / by Christopher L. Harbo.
    p. cm.—(Graphic library. Monster science)
  Summary: "In cartoon format, uses Frankenstein's monster to explain the steps of the scientific method"—Provided by publisher.
  Includes index.
  ISBN 978-1-4296-9931-0 (library binding)
  ISBN 978-1-62065-816-1 (paperback)
  ISBN 978-1-4765-3451-0 (eBook PDF)
1. Science—Methodology—Comic books, strips, etc. 2. Science—Methodology—Juvenile literature.
3. Research—Comic books, strips, etc. 4. Research—Juvenile literature. 5. Graphic novels. I. Title.
II. Series: Graphic library. Monster science.
  Q180.55.M4H37 2014
  001.4′2—dc23   2013006658

Editor
Anthony Wacholtz

Designer
Alison Thiele

Art Director
Nathan Gassman

Production Specialist
Laura Manthe

Printed in the United States of America in Stevens Point, Wisconsin.
032013   007227WZF13

TABLE OF
CONTENTS

CHAPTER 1: METHODS TO THE MADNESS 4

CHAPTER 2: PONDERING QUESTIONS 6

CHAPTER 3: DESIGNING EXPERIMENTS 12

CHAPTER 4: LIGHT FOR LIFE .20

CHAPTER 5: THE END OR JUST THE BEGINNING? 24

GLOSSARY 30
CRITICAL THINKING USING THE COMMON CORE 31
READ MORE 31
INTERNET SITES 32
INDEX 32

METHODS TO THE MADNESS

The world is alive with science.

Everywhere you look, a mystery waits to be unraveled. A problem needs to be solved. A question begs to be answered.

Getting to the bottom of these mysteries may seem tricky. But scientists must be creative and develop ways to solve problems and answer questions.

HEE HEE HEE!

HOW TO DO SCIENCE

This process is sometimes called a scientific method, but there are many ways to answer science questions.

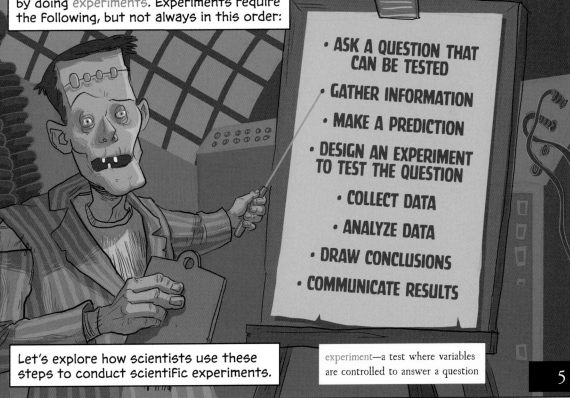

One way scientists answer questions is by doing experiments. Experiments require the following, but not always in this order:

- **ASK A QUESTION THAT CAN BE TESTED**
- **GATHER INFORMATION**
- **MAKE A PREDICTION**
- **DESIGN AN EXPERIMENT TO TEST THE QUESTION**
- **COLLECT DATA**
- **ANALYZE DATA**
- **DRAW CONCLUSIONS**
- **COMMUNICATE RESULTS**

Let's explore how scientists use these steps to conduct scientific experiments.

experiment—a test where variables are controlled to answer a question

CHAPTER 2

PONDERING QUESTIONS

Most scientific investigations begin with a topic you want to learn more about. Ask yourself, what kinds of topics am I interested in?

konk, konk, konk

THINK! THINK!

Choosing a science topic shouldn't strain your brain. Just look around.

The world is full of possibilities. Areas of scientific study include anything in the natural world—animals, people, plants, weather, and so much more.

6

The key is finding something that you are curious about.

I'M CURIOUS ABOUT THE YELLOW LEAVES ON MY LUCKY BAMBOO PLANT.

Excellent! Now that you have a topic, you're ready to figure out what question you have about it.

TO BE, OR NOT TO BE? THAT IS THE QUESTION.

Nice try, but not just any question will do.

Avoid yes-or-no questions that don't take much thought to answer.

POOR QUESTION

IS THE LUCKY BAMBOO PLANT DYING?

variable—something that can change

When scientists do experiments, they ask open-ended questions. These questions can be tested by controlling variables.

GOOD QUESTION

WHAT CAUSES THE LUCKY BAMBOO LEAVES TO TURN YELLOW?

For this question, variables might include the materials the plant grows in or the amount of water it receives.

With your question in hand, you need to research your topic. Maybe someone has already found the answer. Or maybe you need to conduct an investigation.

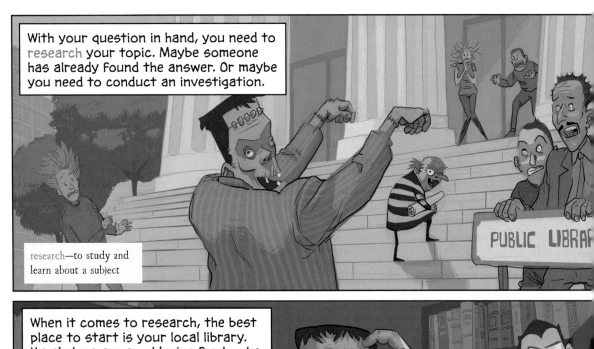

research—to study and learn about a subject

When it comes to research, the best place to start is your local library. Its shelves are a gold mine for books, magazines, and journal articles.

LUCKY BAMBOO'S SCIENTIFIC NAME IS *DRACAENA SANDERIANA*.

DID SOMEONE SAY DRACULA?

In addition to the library, the Internet is also a powerful research tool. Searching for your topic online is bound to bring up dozens of websites just waiting to be explored.

WHOA!

When researching online, always check the source of the information. Not every website online is reliable. Make sure it lists an expert or belongs to a trusted organization.

Beyond books and websites, consider talking to teachers, scientists, or other experts about your topic. Experts may give you information you can't find anywhere else.

NO WAY I'D TRUST THIS SOURCE!

DR. FRANKENSTEIN'S GUIDE TO MAD SCIENCE

TO ANSWER YOUR QUESTION, YES, THIS PLANT CAN FIT A HUMAN IN ITS MOUTH.

DUPLICATE RESEARCH

While researching, you might learn other scientists have already answered your question. In fact, repeating someone else's investigation allows you to see if you get the same results. When a repeated investigation shows the same results, you can be more confident that the results are valid.

ZAP!

valid—based on facts or evidence

9

After researching the topic, you can think about how to answer your question. What do you already know? What variables might influence the result? This information will help you design your experiment.

Making a prediction about what you think will happen can sometimes help you design your experiment. A prediction is often called a hypothesis in science.

HMM ... SHADY AREAS ... DIRECT SUNLIGHT?

DRACAENA SANDERIANA (LUCKY BAMBOO)

• CAN FLOWER IN FALL, WINTER, OR SPRING

• NATIVE TO SHADY AREAS OF RAIN FORESTS

• CAN GROW IN WATER OR SOIL

prediction—a statement of what you think will happen in the future

The key to forming a hypothesis is to make it testable with an experiment.

LUCKY BAMBOO LEAVES WILL STAY GREENER IN INDIRECT SUNLIGHT THAN THEY WILL IN DIRECT SUNLIGHT.

It's elementary! You can test this prediction with an experiment that exposes lucky bamboo to different types of sunlight.

Once you've made your prediction you might worry about whether it's true or false. But don't sweat it. Most predictions are incorrect—and that's OK.

WHEW!

Discovering your prediction is wrong allows you to filter out ideas so you can develop and test new ones.

CHAPTER 3

DESIGNING EXPERIMENTS

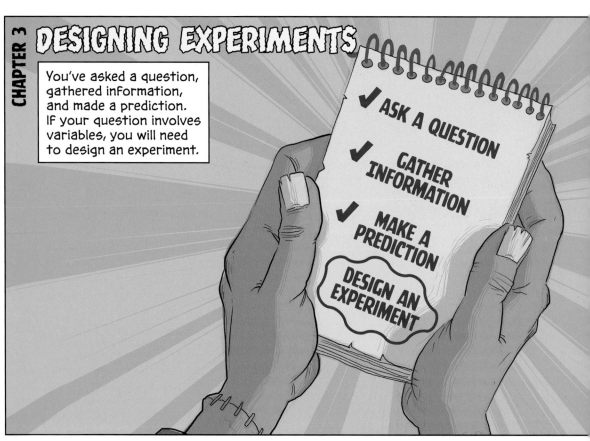

You've asked a question, gathered information, and made a prediction. If your question involves variables, you will need to design an experiment.

✔ ASK A QUESTION

✔ GATHER INFORMATION

✔ MAKE A PREDICTION

DESIGN AN EXPERIMENT

Every experiment has several variables that will affect its outcome. This experiment will test the amount of sunlight to see if it affects leaf color. The only variable that will change is the amount of light.

VARIABLES THAT MIGHT IMPACT PLANT LEAF COLOR:

• AMOUNT OF SUNLIGHT

• AMOUNT OF WATER

• TYPE OF WATER

• TYPE OF SOIL

• TYPE OF CONTAINER

MAY I TAKE YOUR ORDER?

I'M SORRY, SIR. SUNLIGHT IS THE ONLY CHOICE WE HAVE TODAY.

All other variables are off the menu. They are called controlled variables because they stay the same.

Keeping controlled variables exactly the same during your experiment is important. It helps ensure the results of your experiment aren't affected by a change you didn't intend.

OOPS! THAT MIGHT AFFECT OUR RESULTS.

YA THINK?!

The outcome of the experiment will be based on changing the variable being tested, while controlling all the others. For the lucky bamboo, the outcome to look at will be the color of its leaves.

Once you understand the variables of your experiment, it's time to develop a procedure.

ARE YOU SURE THIS IS THE RIGHT KIND OF PROCEDURE?

In this case, a procedure is a plan for conducting the experiment.

One part of a procedure is making a detailed list of the materials and equipment. You'll use it as a checklist for gathering everything you need before setting up the experiment.

procedure—a plan for doing something

Another part of a procedure is to create step-by-step instructions. The instructions should list everything you plan to do from start to finish so that you don't forget something important.

A well-written procedure also gives you a record you can look back on. The record could be helpful if your experiment doesn't turn out the way you expected.

EXPERIMENT PROCEDURE

1. PLACE EACH LUCKY BAMBOO PLANT IN TALL GLASS VASE.

2. PLACE PEBBLES AROUND EACH PLANT'S ROOTS

3. ADD 2 CUPS (480 ML) OF DISTILLED WATER TO EACH VASE.

WAS THAT PART OF YOUR PLAN, MASTER?

You can double-check the procedure to see if you forgot an important variable or overlooked a step.

RECREATING THE EXPERIMENT

A detailed procedure doesn't just help you. It also helps other scientists who want to recreate the experiment in the future. Being able to recreate the experiment allows others to see if your results were accurate.

Once you gather materials and write a procedure, you're ready to conduct your experiment.

When conducting your experiment, follow your procedure exactly. Doing so ensures that the results you get accurately reflect the experiment you planned.

But what if your plan has a flaw? Sometimes the procedure you wrote needs to be changed to make the experiment run smoothly.

CAN YOU GIVE ME A HAND?

JUST THE HAND OR THE WHOLE ARM?

CLUNK

If you make any changes, record them carefully so you can update your procedure.

USE STRONGER THREAD IN STEP 54.

CLUNK

It's also very important to pay close attention to your variables during your experiment.

IGOR, KEEP AN EYE ON THE WATER LEVELS.

Remember, only the variable you are testing can change. The controlled variables must always remain as similar as possible.

YES, MASTER.

During the experiment, you need to make careful measurements and observations. Have a notebook handy to record all of your observations.

observation—a detail you have noticed by using your senses

For general observations during your experiment, make journal entries describing what you see happening.

DAY 10

- SIX LEAVES AND THE STALK OF PLANT A HAVE TURNED YELLOW.

- TWO LEAVES ON THE RIGHT SIDE OF PLANT B HAVE SOME YELLOWING.

- ALL OF THE LEAVES OF PLANT C ARE GREEN AND HEALTHY LOOKING.

- IGOR IS GETTING ON MY NERVES.

Some observations may include numbers and measurements. You can create a table to record the information in a neat and orderly fashion.

Recording data isn't just about what you can write down. A visual record of your experiment might also be important. Cameras and video cameras can come in handy for a few photos or videos of your experiment in action.

data—information collected in an investigation

CHAPTER 4

LIGHT FOR LIFE

You've collected data from your experiment, but now what do you do with it? It's time to analyze your data.

OOPS!

Analyzing a mountain of data may sound overwhelming.

UNNNGHHH!

analyze—to examine something carefully in order to understand it

But it just involves reviewing and organizing the information you've gathered to figure out what it means.

I PROMISE TO BE MORE CAREFUL, MASTER!

Depending on the experiment you conducted, analyzing data may also involve calculating numbers and drawing graphs.

TYPES OF GRAPHS

The three most common graphs for analyzing data are line, bar, and pie graphs. Line graphs show how something changes over time. Bar graphs are useful when you want to compare two or more sets of data. Pie graphs help you show the various parts of a whole set of data.

LINE GRAPH

BAR GRAPH

PIE GRAPH

MMMM ... PIE!

calculate—to find a solution by using math

Once you have analyzed the data, you're ready to draw a conclusion.

HOW DO YOU DRAW A CONCLUSION?

conclusion—a decision or realization based on the facts available

Actually, a conclusion is an explanation based on the data you gathered during the experiment. A conclusion states whether or not the results of your experiment support your prediction.

LUCKY BAMBOO LEAVES STAY GREENER IN INDIRECT SUNLIGHT THAN IN DIRECT SUNLIGHT.

Your conclusion should be supported with evidence from the data you collected. It doesn't matter if your prediction is correct or not. The important thing is that you learned something about the variable you tested.

OH, YEAH!

Sometimes the results of an experiment are due to a variable we hadn't thought about. Or maybe differences we see just naturally occur that way. Scientists often repeat experiments and increase sample sizes so they are more confident with their conclusions.

IGOR, LOOKS LIKE WE NEED MORE LUCKY BAMBOO.

YES, MASTER.

But what if your conclusion doesn't support your prediction? Don't worry, your experiment wasn't a failure. Remember, a false prediction allows you to rethink your ideas and develop a new prediction to test.

OH, THE HORROR!

NON-EXPERIMENTAL SCIENCE

Not all questions can be answered by doing experiments and controlling variables. Do birds eat more before snowstorms? What planets have moons? These kinds of questions require observations instead of experiments. Observational science has broadened our knowledge of the natural world. Scientists keep careful records of what they observe. They also look for patterns.

23

CHAPTER 5

THE END OR JUST THE BEGINNING?

You've analyzed your data and developed a conclusion, but what do you do with that information?

YOU MEAN I'M NOT DONE?!

Not quite. Scientists communicate their results with others.

... AND THOSE WERE MY RESULTS.

VERY INTERESTING.

communicate—to share information, thoughts, or feelings

Communicating results allows other scientists to learn from your findings. It also lets them repeat your experiments to see if they get the same results.

THAT'S GOING TO LEAVE A MARK.

SORRY ABOUT THAT.

POOF!

One way to communicate your results is to write a lab report. This clearly written document explains why and how you conducted the investigation. It includes your analysis, results, and conclusion. Scientists sometimes send their reports to journals for other scientists to read.

A well-written lab report usually includes the following parts:

- ○ TITLE
- ○ PURPOSE
- ○ QUESTION INVESTIGATED
- ○ PREDICTION MADE
- ○ EQUIPMENT AND MATERIALS
- ○ PROCEDURE
- ○ DATA COLLECTED
- ○ RESULTS
- ○ CONCLUSION

Lab reports aren't the only way to communicate results. When sharing results with a group of people or at a science fair, a project display may be in order.

PURPOSE

QUESTION INVESTIGAT

PREDICTION MADE

MATERIALS AND EQUIPM

A

B

A project display includes everything you'd include in a lab report. The difference is the pieces are pasted to a three-panel board or on a large poster.

The way you organize the information on your board or poster can vary depending on your project. The biggest key is to keep your information neat and orderly.

MULTIMEDIA PRESENTATIONS

Computer slide shows and online presentations are additional ways scientists communicate results. Good organization is the key to successful multimedia presentations. Give each part of your report its own slide. Keep your information brief. Include videos and web links that will support your presentation.

Communicating your results is an important part of science. But your scientific investigation may have only just begun.

The results you find in one investigation often lead you to more questions that need to be answered.

WHAT HAPPENS IF YOU GROW A LUCKY BAMBOO IN SOIL INSTEAD OF ROCKS?

GLOSSARY

analyze (AN-uh-lize)—to examine something carefully in order to understand it

calculate (KAL-kyuh-layt)—to find a solution by using math

communicate (kuh-MYOO-nuh-kate)—to share information, thoughts, or feelings

conclusion (kuhn-KLOO-shuhn)—a decision or realization based on the facts available

data (DAY-tuh)—information collected in an investigation

experiment (ik-SPEER-uh-muhnt)—a test where variables are controlled to answer a question

hypothesis (hye-POTH-uh-siss)—a prediction that can be tested about how a scientific investigation or experiment will turn out

investigation (in-vess-tuh-GAY-shuhn)—the search for facts to solve a problem or answer a question

observation (ob-zur-VAY-shuhn)—a detail you have noticed by using your senses

prediction (pri-DIK-shuhn)—a statement of what you think will happen in the future; a hypothesis is a scientific prediction

procedure (pruh-SEE-jur)—a set way of doing something

research (REE-surch)—to study and learn about a subject

variable (VAIR-ee-uh-buhl)—something that can change

CRITICAL THINKING USING THE COMMON CORE

1. What tools does Frankenstein's Monster use to make observations during the experiment? How is he able to use the data he collects to draw conclusions? (Key Ideas)

2. Look at the chart in the top panel on page 19. How would you classify this type of chart? Why is it useful? What other type of chart could you use to show the same information? (Craft and Structure)

3. What is causing the lucky bamboo leaves to turn yellow? How do you know? (Integration of Knowledge and Ideas)

READ MORE

Benbow, Ann, and Colin Mably. *Master the Scientific Method with Fun Life Science Projects.* Real Life Science Experiments. Berkeley Heights, N.J.: Enslow Publishers, 2010.

Burns, Kylie. *What's the Problem?: How to Start Your Scientific Investigation.* Step into Science. New York: Crabtree Pub., 2010.

Chappell, Rachel M. *Solving Science Questions: A Book about the Scientific Process.* Big Ideas for Young Scientists. Vero Beach, Fla.: Rourke Pub., 2008.

Lemke, Donald B. *Investigating the Scientific Method with Max Axiom, Super Scientist.* Graphic Science. Mankato, Minn.: Capstone Press, 2008.

INTERNET SITES

FactHound offers a safe, fun way to find Internet sites related to this book. All sites on FactHound have been researched by our staff.

Here's all you do:

Visit www.facthound.com

Type in this code: 9781429699310

Super-cool stuff! Check out projects, games and lots more at www.capstonekids.com

INDEX

analyzing data, 20–21, 22, 24

communicating results, 24–28
conclusions, 22, 23, 24, 25

data, 19, 20, 21, 22, 24
designing experiments, 12–15
developing questions, 6–7

graphs, 21

hypotheses, 10, 11

lab reports, 25, 26–27
libraries, 8

multimedia, 27

non-experimental science, 23

observations, 18, 19, 23

predictions, 10, 11, 12, 22, 23
procedures, 14, 15, 16, 17, 29

repeating experiments, 15, 23
research, 8–9

tables, 19

variables, 7, 10, 12, 13, 14, 23